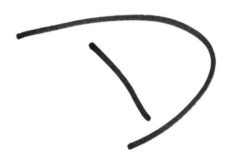

WOMEN WHO WIN

Cynthia Cooper

Mia Hamm

Martina Hingis

Chamique Holdsclaw

Michelle Kwan

Lisa Leslie

Sheryl Swoopes

Venus & Serena Williams

CHELSEA HOUSE PUBLISHERS

WOMEN WHO WIN

CHAMIQUE HOLDSCLAW

Kay Cornelius

Introduction by
HANNAH STORM

CHELSEA HOUSE PUBLISHERS
Philadelphia

Frontis: *Considered by many to be the best female basketball player in the world, Chamique Holdsclaw holds the WNBA 1999 Rookie of the Year Award, one of the scores of honors she has received throughout her basketball career.*

Produced by
21st Century Publishing and Communications, Inc.
New York, New York
http://www.21cpc.com

CHELSEA HOUSE PUBLISHERS

Editor in Chief: Stephen Reginald
Managing Editor: James D. Gallagher
Production Manager: Pamela Loos
Art Director: Sara Davis
Director of Photography: Judy L. Hasday
Senior Production Editor: J. Christopher Higgins
Publishing Coordinator: James McAvoy
Project Editor: Anne Hill

The Chelsea House World Wide Web address is
http://www.chelseahouse.com

First Printing

1 3 5 7 9 8 6 4 2

Library of Congress Cataloging-in-Publication Data

Cornelius, Kay.
   Chamique Holdsclaw / Kay Cornelius; introduction by Hannah Storm.
   p. cm. – (Women who win)
   Includes bibliographical references (p.) and index.
   Summary: Presents a biography of the star player for the Washington Mystics
of the Women's National Basketball Association.
   ISBN 0-7910-5793-3 (hc) — ISBN 0-7910-6153-1 (pbk)
   1. Holdsclaw, Chamique—Juvenile literature. 2. Basketball players—United States—
Biography—Juvenile literature. 3. Women basketball players—United States—
Biography—Juvenile literature. [1. Holdsclaw, Chamique. 2. Basketball players.
3. Women—Biography. 4. Afro-Americans—Biography.] I. Title. II. Series.

GV884.H63 C67 2001
796.323'092—dc21
[B]   00—022720
                                                              CIP
                                                               AC

Contents

Introduction   6

Chapter 1
Mike and "Meek"   9

Chapter 2
"She's a Girl, She Stinks"   17

Chapter 3
"Meek" Rocks Rocky Top   25

Chapter 4
"Cha-Mi-Que!"   37

Chapter 5
A Different Kind of Game   47

Chapter 6
Winning Ways   55

Statistics   60
Chronology   61
Further Reading   62
Index   64

WOMEN WHO WIN

Hannah Storm
NBC Studio Host

Y̲ou go girl! Women's sports are the hottest thing going right now, with the 1900s ending in a big way. When the U.S. team won the 1999 Women's World Cup, it captured the imagination of all sports fans and served as a great inspiration for young girls everywhere to follow their dreams.

That was just the exclamation point on an explosive decade for women's sports—capped off by the Olympic gold medals for the U.S. women in hockey, softball, and basketball. All the excitement created by the U.S. national basketball team helped to launch the Women's National Basketball Association (WNBA), which began play in 1997. The fans embraced the concept, and for the first time, a successful and stable women's professional basketball league was formed.

I was the first ever play-by-play announcer for the WNBA—a big personal challenge. Broadcasting, just like sports, had some areas with limited opportunities for women. There have traditionally not been many play-by-play opportunities for women in sports television, so I had no experience. To tell you the truth, the challenge I faced was a little scary! Sometimes we are all afraid that we might not be up to a certain task. It is not easy to take risks, but unless we push ourselves we will stagnate and not grow.

Here's what happened to me. I had always wanted to do play-by-play earlier in my career, but I had never gotten the opportunity. Not that I was unhappy— I had been given studio hosting assignments that were unprecedented for a woman and my reputation was well established in the business. I was comfortable in my role . . . plus I had just had my first baby. The last thing I needed to do was suddenly tackle a new skill on national television and risk being criticized (not to mention, very stressed out!). Although I had always wanted to do play-by-play, I turned down the assignment twice, before reluctantly agreeing to give it a try. During my hosting stint of the NBA finals that year, I traveled back and forth to WNBA preseason games to practice play-by-play. I was on 11 flights in 14 days to seven different cities! My head was spinning and it was no surprise that I got sick. On the day of the first broadcast, I had to have shots just so I could go on the air without throwing up. I felt terrible and nervous, but

6

I survived my first game. I wasn't very good but gradually, week by week, I got better. By the end of the season, the TV reviews of my work were much better—*USA Today* called me "most improved."

During that 1997 season, I witnessed a lot of exciting basketball moments, from the first historic game to the first championship, won by the Houston Comets. The challenge of doing play-by-play was really exciting and I loved interviewing the women athletes and seeing the fans' enthusiasm. Over one million fans came to the games; my favorite sight was seeing young boys wearing the jerseys of female players—pretty cool. And to think I almost missed out on all of that. It reinforced the importance of taking chances and not being afraid of challenges or criticism. When we have an opportunity to follow our dreams, we need to go for it!

Thankfully, there are now more opportunities than ever for women in sports (and other areas, like broadcasting). We thank women, like those in this series, who have persevered despite lack of opportunities—women who have refused to see their limitations. Remember, women's sports has been around a long time. Way back in 396 B.C. Kyniska, a Spartan princess, won an Olympic chariot race. Of course, women weren't allowed to compete, so she was not allowed to collect her prize in person. At the 1996 Olympic games in Atlanta, Georgia, over 35,600 women competed, almost a third more than in the previous Summer Games. More than 20 new women's events have been added for the Sydney, Australia, Olympics in 2000. Women's collegiate sports continues to grow, spurred by the 1972 landmark legislation Title IX, which states that "no person in the United States shall, on the basis of sex, be excluded from participation in, be denied the benefits of, or be subjected to discrimination under any educational program or activity receiving federal financial assistance." This has set the stage for many more scholarships and opportunities for women, and now we have professional leagues as well. No longer do the most talented basketball players in the country have to go to Europe or Asia to earn a living.

The women in this series did not have as many opportunities as you have today. But they were persistent through all obstacles, both on the court and off. I can tell you that Cynthia Cooper is the strongest woman I know. What is it that makes Cynthia and the rest of the women included in this series so special? They are not afraid to share their struggles and their stories with us. Their willingness to show us their emotions, open their hearts, bare their souls, and let us into their lives is what, in my mind, separates them from their male counterparts. So accept this gift of their remarkable stories and be inspired. Because *you*, too, have what it takes to follow your dreams.

1

MIKE AND "MEEK"

Hoops star Michael Jordan, whose name is known worldwide, is probably the most famous basketball player of all time. Even people who never attend games or pay attention to the sport have seen him on television commercials and in magazine advertisements. Filmgoers can also see him in a movie called *Space Jam*, in which he acted alongside a crowd of cartoon characters.

Jordan's rise to fame began in a North Carolina high school, where he played both guard and forward positions. While forward players are usually the best shooters, guards protect their team's basket and try to keep their opponents from scoring. Guards also defend by getting rebounds— grabbing the ball when the other team misses a shot.

An All-American in college and Player of the Year in 1983–84, Jordan got the nickname "Air" because he seemed to be suspended in the air when he made a jump shot. After college, he played pro ball for the Chicago Bulls and, in his first year, averaged 28 points per game. Jordan was also named Rookie of the Year, which meant that he

Chamique "Meek" Holdsclaw drives the ball down the court. Her power, style, and jumping skills on the court remind many of basketball superstar Michael Jordan, to whom she is often compared.

was the best first-year professional basketball player in the National Basketball Association (NBA). Later, he was the first to be voted both the Most Valuable Player (MVP) and the Defensive Player of the Year.

Basketball players around the world watched Michael Jordan and envied his skill and prowess. Wishing they could play like he did, they tried to copy his moves, which he seemed to make with such little effort. Young hopefuls wanted to be the next Michael Jordan. Year after year passed, however, and no one ever matched Mike's total game.

Then along came a player who some people began calling "the next Michael Jordan." To the surprise of many, it turned out that this exciting new talent was a woman. Chamique (Shuh-MEEK-Wah) Holdsclaw, known as "Meek," is every inch a basketball player, standing at 6' 2" and weighing in at a strong 166 pounds. Her grandmother had hoped she would be a ballerina, but Meek's size-14 shoes ruled out that career. Now her grandmother says that Chamique is "like a ballerina on the court." With just a slight push off one foot, she sails high in the air.

Like Mike, Meek can play both guard and forward. She also plays center, a position often given to the tallest player or the one with the best reach. Centers need long arms and good jumping ability to rebound and to tip the ball toward their teammates during jump-offs. (A jump-off signals the beginning of each half of the game and occurs at other times when the referee calls for a jump ball.) Chamique is also a powerhouse in dribbling, driving, and shooting, at which she is superb using either her left or right hand.

Michael Jordan has no trouble eluding his guards as he makes one of the phenomenal leaps that earned him fame and the nickname "Air" Jordan.

Women like Chamique and many other outstanding players would not have been accepted when women's basketball was first introduced. Although women's games were played at the college level as early as the late 1890s, the sport has a history of struggling to become a recognized, professional game for women. For decades, women's basketball was a genteel sport in which women were expected to behave in a ladylike fashion. Players did not play the full court and were required to stay in their assigned places. Dribbling more than three times, holding the ball for more than three seconds, or snatching the ball from other players was forbidden. Furthermore, women players were burdened by the "fashions" of the times, with long dresses and sleeves and heavy leather shoes.

Despite the restrictions, women continued to play, and women's college teams competed across the country. Rules were changed to conform more to men's regulations, and women's uniforms became less confining. In 1936, the first national, professional women's team was formed. Called the All-American Red Heads, the team used men's rules and played against men. Until the team disbanded in 1986, the All-American Red Heads toured across the United States and even played overseas.

Although U.S. women's amateur teams won championships at Olympic games in the 1970s, '80s, and '90s, the United States still had no professional women's league to match the men's NBA. Women played basketball in high school and college, and if they wanted to play professionally, they had to join teams overseas. Women's college basketball was tremendously popular, however, and when the Women's National Basketball Association (WNBA) was finally formed in 1997, the league chose many of its players from among the best of the college stars.

Chamique Holdsclaw is one of those stars. Like Michael Jordan, she began her rise to basketball fame in high school, and before long she was being compared to "His Airness."

Meek led her high school team to four straight New York State Championships and, like Jordan, went on to master college basketball and to pile up honors and awards.

Chamique has, in fact, collected more awards and won them earlier in her career than did her hero Mike. Jordan made the men's All-American team twice when he was in college; Chamique made the women's All-American team all four of her college years. Mike was named Associated Press (AP) Player of the Year once; Chamique received the same title three years in a row.

Chamique has racked up scores of further honors and titles. In 1998 she won the Honda-Broderick Cup as the outstanding woman college athlete of the year. (The winner is chosen from players in each of 10 competitive sports, including soccer, swimming, basketball, volleyball, and track and field.) She made the Kodak Silver Anniversary Team as one of the 10 best women players of the last 25 years and won a gold medal in the World Basketball Championships.

Adding to her laurels was the 1999 U.S. Basketball Writers' Player of the Year honor and, in the same year, she was selected to play on the U.S. women's basketball team in the 2000 Olympics. Chamique was also chosen as the 1998 and 1999 Naismith Player of the Year Award (named in honor of James Naismith, who invented basketball), and was the first woman basketball player to win the prestigious James E. Sullivan Memorial Award as outstanding amateur athlete of 1998. The award is given to the athlete who, "by his or her performance, example and influence as an amateur, has done the most during the year to advance the cause of sportsmanship." Since the Sullivan Award was first given in 1930, the only other

Chamique signs autographs for a group of young fans. To many boys and girls, she is a hero who has shown how determination and talent can take an athlete to the top.

basketball players to receive it have been Bill Bradley in 1965 and Bill Walton in 1973.

To add to her honors, Chamique was the first player to be chosen in the 1999 WNBA draft by the Washington (D.C.) Mystics. Like Michael Jordan in the NBA, Chamique was named Rookie of the Year in her first season of professional basketball in the WNBA. These two champions also share the same jersey number—23. Being a fan of Mike's had nothing to do with Chamique's choice, however. She took number 23 because it reminds her of her favorite Bible passage, the 23rd Psalm.

Chamique's style also reminds many people of "Air" Jordan. Pat Summitt, her college coach, said that one reason why Meek was the best player on the team was because she could stay aloft for so long after jumping. "Chamique could linger around the glass [the backboard of the goal], while everyone else was jumping, and falling again. . . . There were times when she changed position in midair. She would move, meet an opponent, and seem to shape-shift. Suddenly, there she would be, on the *other* side of the basket, with an open shot."

One *Newsweek* magazine article describes how Chamique "remains calm and fluid, with a dazzling array of spin moves. She likes to play close to the basket, using her long legs to snake through the lane for a layup or rebound." She uses her long arms to throw fall-away jump shots like Michael Jordan's. And M.J. [Michael Jordan] is one of Chamique's greatest admirers. "Meek is fun to watch—exciting with a lot of skills," Mike says. "She'll definitely take women's sports to a new high."

Chamique grew up watching Jordan play, but they met for the first time in January 1998, when her college team visited Michael at his office in Chicago. He knew who she was right away. "What's up, 'Mique?" he asked when he saw her. Then he jokingly challenged Chamique to a game of one-on-one.

A few months later, when a national magazine named Chamique one of the "Women We Love," Jordan had only praise for her, saying, "She is, without a doubt, the most exciting women's basketball player ever."

How did a very skinny, very tall little girl from a housing project grow up to be the most-honored woman basketball player of all time? The answer can be found back where it all began —the Astoria Houses in Queens, New York.

2

"She's a Girl, She Stinks"

Chamique Holdsclaw was born on August 9, 1977, and grew up in the New York City borough of Queens. When her parents separated, the family was broken up, and 11-year-old Chamique moved in with her grandmother, June Holdsclaw. Grandmother Holdsclaw lived in Astoria Houses, a high-rise project, and worked as a hospital clerk. Chamique's brother, Davon, lived with her and June for a time but later moved back with their mother. Chamique, who had grown very attached to her grandmother, decided to stay with her in the Astoria Houses.

The projects don't offer many opportunities for sports, but Astoria Houses did have basketball courts within the complex. Soon, Chamique and her cousin Andrew were visiting them every day, hoping to pick up a game. While Chamique looked on and longed to play, the boys only allowed Andrew on the court. When the games ended, she and Andrew played one-on-one, and soon the older boys began to notice just how good she was.

June Holdsclaw, who had played basketball as a girl,

Chamique shares a moment with her beloved grandmother, June Holdsclaw. From the time she was a child growing up in a housing project through her career as a basketball star, grandmother June has been Chamique's inspiration.

also recognized her granddaughter's talents, especially when she discovered that as an eighth grader, Chamique could hurl the ball from one end of the court to the other. While Chamique was still in grammar school, June encouraged her to join an eight-team league at a local community center, but she was rejected when the boys voted not to allow girls to play.

Chamique was determined, however, and when she persisted with the league director, Tyrone Green, and showed him her dribbling skill, he put her on a team. Playing with a girl did not please the boys, and they took their grievance to Green. "She's a girl, she stinks," they complained. Chamique stayed, however, and soon became the team's leading scorer.

Although proud of Chamique's basketball prowess, June wanted her to enjoy other activities as well. Part of her concern was to keep her granddaughter busy and off the sometimes dangerous streets of their neighborhood. She enrolled Chamique in all kinds of after-school programs, including a glee club, jazz dance, and ballet. Tall and long-legged, Chamique might seem natural as a dancer. It was soon clear to everyone, however, that she would not have much of a career dancing. On the court, she could reach and leap and twist, but her dancing was awkward and ungraceful. Years later, Chamique told her college coach that the dance teacher could have hit her with a stick, and she still wouldn't be able to do the ballet stretches.

June was a warm, loving grandparent, but she had firm rules that she expected her granddaughter to obey. Chamique was not allowed to hang around on the streets and had to be home after dark. Every Sunday they attended the local

Lutheran church, where June admonished her granddaughter to "sit up straight." June made her rules clear to Chamique saying, "As long as you live in my house you go to school and to church, you don't sit around, and you aren't out on the street."

With all her activities, especially her basketball, it was unlikely that Chamique would spend much time on the streets. For Chamique, basketball seemed to be an obsession. She played every afternoon, all year round, even in the winter, when she shoveled snow from the court to play. She stayed on the court as long as her grandmother would let her, and even if no one was around for a pick-up game, she shot scores of baskets by herself. Around the Astoria Houses, Chamique was known as "Flat Out" because

Courts like this one were the training ground for young Chamique. Obsessed with basketball, she spent every spare moment practicing her game and taking on any and all boys who were willing to play ball with a girl.

she would flat out stop anything else to play basketball. As she told magazine reporters in later years, "Big boys, small boys, whoever, I was always ready to take them on. I wasn't scared of anybody's game."

One of the boys who played with Chamique on their neighborhood Boys and Girls Club team was Ron Artest, who went on to become a college basketball star himself. He remembers how Chamique played on their team: "It was crazy how good she was. She could slap the backboard. When you're 12 or 13, that's like dunking."

In grammar school, where Chamique was called the "Skinny One," she helped her school take on all comers and win a basketball championship. When it was time for high school, everyone thought she would go to St. John's Prep, a well-known school near her home with a good basketball program. Then she heard that Christ the King High School had the best girls' program in the city and that decided it for her. June also approved of Christ the King because she knew that many girls from the high school had received athletic scholarships. She was anxious for Chamique to go on to college and get a solid education, perhaps even become a teacher.

Alerted by Tyrone Green, Christ the King coach Vinny Cannizzaro decided to visit the Astoria courts and watch this eighth-grader play. Completely surprised at how good Chamique already was, he signed her up. Although attending Christ the King meant a long bus ride every day, Chamique endured the trip because she was determined to play on a team that had a chance to win a championship.

Chamique played for Christ the King all four

of her high school years, and the girls' basketball team was New York State high school champion for each of those four years. During that time the team had a record of 106 wins and only four losses. In her final season, Chamique averaged 25 points and 15 rebounds to become the best scorer and rebounder the school had ever had. Describing Chamique's talents, Coach Cannizzaro enthused, "We've been blessed with a lot of great players, but she has to be the best."

Long hours at school and being a champion player were still not enough for Chamique. She looked for chances to play basketball around the courts in Queens, going up against all comers, including grown men. She played hard and strong, and even if she didn't always win, she definitely impressed her opponents. At 16, Chamique won a three-point shooting contest

The halls of Christ the King High School, where Chamique led her team to four state championships, are adorned with the memorabilia of the school's basketball victories. The high school's program has produced one of the nation's largest group of college and professional basketball stars.

against some of the best teenage boys in New York City, and by the time she was a junior in high school, offers of scholarships to play college basketball began pouring in.

In recruiting players, college coaches travel to high schools and interview prospects, hoping they can talk the best players into joining their teams. One coach, Pat Summitt of the University of Tennessee, had never recruited a New York player before. She didn't really think that a big-city girl would want to come to a small city like Knoxville, Tennessee. Summitt doubted that her school had any chance at all of getting Chamique. Then, in September 1994, after talking to Chamique's grandmother on the telephone, Pat Summitt and her assistant flew to New York.

In *Raise the Roof*, a book by Pat Summitt about Tennessee's championship seasons, the women's basketball coach tells what happened the first time Chamique saw her in person. "I had on a tailored suit, a pair of high heels that made me over six feet tall, and vivid red lipstick," Pat Summitt writes. "You look fake!" Chamique told her. The coach replied that she was very real and that she wanted Chamique to join the Tennessee team. On hearing the coach's Southern accent, Chamique put her hand over her mouth and burst into what Pat Summitt calls Chamique's "whoop-whoop-whoop giggles." Then Chamique asked Pat and her assistant some of the questions she had asked coaches from other schools. Would she be a starting player as a freshman? How much playing time would she get?

It is common for many coaches to offer enticing deals to prospective players, and other schools had made such offers and promises to

Chamique, but the Tennessee coach did not. "I've never promised a player a starting job, and I never will," Pat Summitt told her. "Are you *ready* to play in front of 25,000 people?" she asked. Summitt also told Chamique, "I'll make you the best player you can be. If you work hard, you'll see it." Chamique later told Pat Summitt that she was glad the coach had not made promises. She had always liked a challenge.

June Holdsclaw also liked what she heard from the coach. Being from Alabama, June felt at home with the Southern accents, but more importantly she approved of the way Tennessee ran its basketball program. When the interview was over, June told Chamique, "They're strict. I don't allow a lot of coming and going, and they don't either."

So it was settled. The tall, lanky girl with braces on her teeth and size-14 basketball shoes on her feet, who could have played basketball at almost any college in the country, had found a new home. And in Chamique Holdsclaw, the Tennessee basketball program had found a bright new star.

3

"MEEK" ROCKS ROCKY TOP

T he University of Tennessee sits on a series of hills in Knoxville, only a few miles from the Great Smoky Mountain National Park. Students call their campus Rocky Top and play the song "Rocky Top" during football and basketball games. Tennessee itself is known as the Volunteer State, a name it received in tribute to the tens of thousands of Tennesseans who volunteered to serve their country in every war since the American Revolution. It seemed only natural then that male athletes who played for the university should be known as the Vols. When the women's basketball team was formed, it was called the Lady Vols.

By the time Chamique arrived on the college campus, the University of Tennessee Lady Vols had already won three National College Athletic Association (NCAA) basketball championships and were looking for more. A star on her grammar and high school teams, Chamique was now one of several players on a team that already worked well together. She knew that going to a university and playing

---

At the University of Tennessee, Chamique, conferring here with team coach Pat Summitt, rocked the college with her triumphant four-year career. She made the school's history books as the leading scorer and rebounder, prompting Coach Summitt to remark, "there is only one Chamique."

for the Lady Vols would be different.

The city of Knoxville was also very different for Chamique. She thought it was quite odd that Knoxville's residents seemed to be either black or white. As a young woman from an integrated neighborhood in Queens, she was used to seeing different ethnic groups. Where, she wondered, were the Latinos and Asians? At the university, like other freshmen, she had to study very hard to keep up with her school work. Unlike many other freshmen, however, Chamique also had to play ball and prove to the coaches and her teammates she could play their kind of game.

Coach Pat Summitt says she didn't fully understand what kind of player the team was getting until she saw Chamique in action for herself the first time. During Chamique's first freshman practice, she played alone against three male players, and Summitt later described the encounter: "I watched closely, interested to see what she would do. . . . She feigned [faked] to her left, dribbled behind her back, then cut right. She split the first two guys and ran right between them. That left one defender between her and the basket. Driving down the lane and directly at the basket, she met up with the lone player, switched hands, blew right by her opponent, and went up for a reverse layup. She spun, and kissed the ball neatly off the glass."

Everyone on the court stopped dead in their tracks and stared, motionless, in disbelief at Chamique, their jaws dropping. They had not expected a new freshman to take on male players at her first practice. And they certainly did not expect that this newcomer would make the men look bad.

It was clear that the young freshman was an exceptional player and was confident in her abilities. Nevertheless, she still had to follow the coaches' instructions. Like most coaches, Summitt and her staff often raised their voices to the players, yelling and hollering at practice and in games. Chamique, who had never met a coach like Summitt, was not used to such treatment and was not sure whether or not she liked her.

The coaches were not sure what to make of

Located in Knoxville, the University of Tennessee, with its large campus and many buildings was strange at first to the young athlete from Queens. Chamique adjusted, however, and found she was very much at home on the school's basketball court.

Chamique, either. Pat Summitt tells of a time in Chamique's freshman year when the Lady Vols had lost a tough game. While the coaches were talking about the terrible play of their team, they heard Chamique giggling. "Maybe you can explain just what's so funny?" an assistant coach demanded, and Chamique burst into tears. Laughing or giggling, they discovered later, was how Chamique reacted when she was upset.

Chamique survived her freshman year, however, and also had an excellent first season. She averaged 12.7 points and eight rebounds in her first three games and was named the Southeastern Conference Player of the Week. In one week of play in January, the Lady Vols beat Louisiana Tech, which was then ranked first in the nation, and went on to beat the number-two-ranked Commodores of Vanderbilt University. Finally, they won against Arkansas. In those three games, Chamique averaged 20.3 points and 11 rebounds and was also named college basketball Player of the Week by ESPN, the first woman to earn that honor. Chamique guided her team to the NCAA championship that year and was the only freshman to be named one of the 10 Kodak All-American players.

One example that proved Chamique's value to her team occurred when the Lady Vols played Georgia during a Southeastern Conference game. The Lady Vols were 11 points behind with less than three minutes to go. In the time left, Chamique scored 15 points, 9 of which were three-point shots (goals made farther from the basket count a point more). The teams were tied when time ran out. In overtime, Chamique scored 8 of Tennessee's

With her signature leap, Chamique towers over her opponents to sink a basket during a championship game with Louisiana Tech. With the talent to play forward, guard, and center, Chamique dominates the court from any position.

12 points, and the Lady Vols won.

Her impressive performance brought high praise from her high school coach, Vincent Cannizarro, who commented. "I imagined she'd make a positive contribution as a freshman, but I don't think anybody envisioned her accomplishing what she did."

Although Chamique's teammates were glad to have a player like her on their side on the court, they were not about to let her forget that she was still only a lowly freshman off the court. On their first road trip to Hawaii for the Kona Classic, her teammates presented her with a yellow broomstick before the flight and told her it was the "freshman pole" and that she would have to carry it during the trip. Thinking it was a tradition she could not break, the unsuspecting freshman dutifully carried the broomstick through the airport and onto the plane. A coach finally told her the others were just teasing her. The Lady Vols enjoyed the joke so much that from then on it indeed became a tradition that freshmen would take turns carrying the "pole" to the first game away from home. Tennessee won the Kona Classic title—and Chamique earned Most Valuable Player honors.

Despite her success, however, the relationship between Chamique and Pat Summitt was at times quite tense. At the start of Chamique's sophomore season, the coach took her aside and told her that she needed to improve her practice habits. Chamique's feelings were so hurt that she threatened to give it all up. Tears streaming down her face, she blurted to Summitt, "I hate it here, I'm leaving."

Upset and hurt, Chamique phoned June Holdsclaw, who had no intention of accepting her granddaughter's decision. In no uncertain terms, June admonished Chamique, "When you walked out my door, you made a decision. I expect you to stay there for four years. You're graduating from Tennessee."

Chamique could not oppose her beloved grandmother. She stayed at Tennessee, and as the year progressed, her relationship with Pat Summitt improved as well, especially when the coach praised her as the best player she had ever coached. Describing Chamique's skills, Summitt said that she played "as if she had hinges in her arms and legs." She could twist and turn her way to get the ball into the basket; she could reverse her position on a dime and then make a second effort to get a tip-in. Coach Summitt also noted that after a hard-played game, Chamique often did not seem to realize how well she had done and was surprised to hear how many points she had scored. But more than once, Chamique's skill and determination guided her team to a win.

Chamique continued her phenomenal play on into her sophomore year. Once more, led by Chamique, the Lady Vols won the national championship, and once again Chamique made the Kodak All-American team. She was also named Most Valuable Player in the Final Four, the top four teams that meet to decide the national championship.

By the time she was a junior, Chamique had moved out of the dormitory and into her own apartment off campus. The pressure of being in the spotlight for two years was taking its toll on her, and she felt she needed the privacy. Chamique also paid less attention to the freshmen on her team, and some of them resented her for it. As tensions mounted, freshman

A triumphant Chamique shows off the National Collegiate Championship trophy she and her teammates won in Chamique's junior year at Tennessee.

Tamika Catchings let Chamique know how disappointed she was with her. "You were the person that I was so excited to come here and play with. But now that I know how you are, I don't know if I want to be friends with you." The incident was smoothed over when the teammates talked it through and realized that the team would fall apart if they allowed dissension among themselves.

A big part of the problem was pressure from agents, who persisted in contacting Chamique to tempt and persuade her to leave college and become a professional basketball player. They made lucrative offers and great promises. As a professional, she would certainly make a lot of money, not only from playing but also from endorsing products. Some agents also tried to get to her through her friends; others plagued her with nonstop telephone calls or even showed up at the university to try and interview her. Chamique had to learn to be suspicious of everyone.

It was no secret that Chamique welcomed a challenge, and because the Lady Vols were winning nearly all their games, it would not be surprising if Chamique became bored. Turning professional would be a great challenge and would also bring her the money to move her grandmother away from the housing projects.

Making a decision was a difficult struggle for Chamique, but she was reminded of her grandmother's ambition for her—that she would graduate from the university. She also knew that every Lady Vol is expected to complete her four years. Finally, Coach Summitt made it clear to Chamique that she had to make up her mind about her future. "Everyone thinks I'm leaving, but right now I want to stay and get my degree," she explained to Summitt. "I don't want to be the one to set a negative trend, instead of a positive one. I don't want to be the player who brings it down a notch."

Having finally resolved the tough question of returning to school for her senior year, Chamique continued her junior year with an even more outstanding season than her first two. Once more, the Lady Vols easily won the national basketball title with a perfect season of 30 wins and no losses. Chamique was named the Final Four's MVP, and she made the Kodak All-American team again.

Chamique had garnered these honors before, but now she was winning others. The AP voted her Player of the Year, and she was awarded the Honda-Broderick Cup. Her most important award, however, was the James E. Sullivan Memorial Award. In winning this prestigious honor, she followed in the footsteps of another University of Tennessee athlete, football player Peyton Manning, who was the 1997 winner.

In the press conference after the game that brought the Lady Vols their third straight championship, Chamique told reporters that she would come back the next year to try to help Tennessee win a fourth national title, which would be a first for any team. "I will be back at Tennessee. It's firm, and it's final," she asserted.

To top off that exceptional season, during the spring and summer, Chamique played on the U.S. Women's Basketball Team in the World Championships. The only college player on a team of professional players, she helped the United States win the event and bring home the gold medal.

After three impressive years at Tennessee, Chamique looked forward to even more challenges in her senior year. During her final college year, the young star would discover something important about herself and make significant decisions about her future.

4

"CHA-MI-QUE!"

January 3, 1999, was a cold, windy day in New York City. The harsh weather could not keep more than 15,000 screaming fans away from Madison Square Garden, however. That night, the Garden was hosting a women's college basketball game between New Jersey's Rutgers University and the University of Tennessee. The match was unique because Rutgers and Tennessee would not normally play each other in New York City. It was Coach Summitt who had arranged the game's location as a sort of "thank you" for what Chamique had meant to the Lady Vols. After a rough start, the coach and Chamique had come to admire and respect each other.

A good share of the crowd was there for one reason—to see Chamique Holdsclaw in action. As she moved onto the court to warm up with her teammates, the chanting began. From every corner of the arena, the cries rang out.

"Cha-mi-que! Cha-mi-que!"

"Meek!"

"Meek-a!"

A fan favorite, when Chamique displays her hoops prowess, she can be assured her admirers will greet her with cheers and shouts of encouragement. One of the greatest college athletes of all time, she finished her final year at Tennessee with a record 3,025 points.

Two other women on the team—Semeka Randall and Tamika Catchings—had also gotten the nicknames "Meek." But Chamique was definitely the "home girl," the one Meek that so many fans had come out to welcome that night. The game could have been called Holdsclaw's Homecoming, since it was Chamique's first chance to play in New York City. Many in the stands were friends and former teammates she grew up with who had turned out to see the most honored player in women's basketball. Long before Chamique had left New York for Tennessee, her admirers knew her as a winner. No team she had played on had ever had a losing season thanks in large part to her outstanding skills as both a scorer and defensive player.

Stepping onto the court that night, Chamique had quite a reputation to live up to. Relatives, friends, and former teammates were there to cheer her on. She tried not to think about where she was or who might be watching. Most importantly, she was confident and ready to give her best to the game she had always loved. As the starting whistle blew, Chamique, her hair pulled back from her face, took her usual spot on the floor and crouched for the tip-off. She was all business.

When the two teams met that night in New York, Tennessee was number one in the nation; Rutgers was ranked 15. Despite what might have seemed to be an easy win for the Lady Vols, their star player did not do well in scoring, playing one of her poorest offensive games. Perhaps playing before so many eager fans and friends put too much pressure on Chamique. Her timing seemed off, and she drove home only eight points and had just nine rebounds. She did, however, play an excellent defensive game, and Tennessee went on to win 68-54.

Although disappointed in her scoring, her team had won, and Chamique was excited that such a crowd turned out to see it happen. A record was broken that night; more people had come to Madison Square Garden to see a college women's basketball game than ever before. "This is awesome. Fifteen thousand people," Chamique said enthusiastically. "It's awesome. I would never have dreamt that this many people would be here for a women's basketball game."

Chamique made no excuses for her own lack of scoring, but Pat Summitt understood how hard it must have been for Chamique to play at home in front of so many people she knew. "She may have put a bit more pressure on herself to do well here at home," the coach explained.

Although the game was among Chamique's worst ever, she was not disheartened. She made it clear that she still believed in her ability to play. In her usual soft voice, without bragging, she said, "I know I can get 30 points the next night. The sky's the limit."

Certainly the huge number of fans who crowded the Garden that night proved that people wanted to watch women's basketball. Chamique knew that the professional WNBA team New York Liberty was eager to sign her up when she finished college. She had always thought it would be great to return to New York to play professional ball. "Madison Square Garden is just fifteen minutes from my house!" she explained. It would be an easy subway ride for grandmother June, the most important person in Chamique's life, to get to the games.

The more Chamique thought about it, however, the more she began to have doubts. Playing in the Garden that night helped her realize that New York might not be the best place for her. Along with the tremendous pressure to excel, the very people she had known for years could be a distraction. Chamique knew she had to focus totally on her game. "I learned a lesson when I played in Madison Square Garden," she told one reporter. "Your friends want tickets, they want to be with you, and I don't need that right now. I'm trying to establish my own life."

After the Rutgers game, when someone pointed out that Chamique had made only eight points, she promised, "That won't happen again." It didn't. The next week, the Lady Vols had a tough game against the University of Connecticut. The Connecticut Huskies had won 54 straight games at home and had reached the rank of number one. Tennessee, meanwhile had slipped to number two. With the game tied at 76 and a little more than three minutes remaining to play, Tennessee won, thanks in part to Chamique's 25 points, nine rebounds, and four assists.

Discussing Chamique's extraordinary play, the Huskies' coach recalled, "I don't remember her getting an easy shot in the second half, where she just squared up and shot with nobody near her. Every shot she took, there were people there. . . . She's a great player who makes tough shots, and that's what great players do."

The Lady Vols still had to play many other games to finish the season, and they faced

Bruises, bumps, and pulled muscles are all part of playing hard and strong. Benched in the final minutes of a game against Florida, Chamique talks with Coach Summitt as she ices her sore knee.

tough opposition. Every team they played was determined to snatch away their three-year title as NCAA champions. Games were fast and hard. Players often hit the floor fighting for the ball, and cuts, bruises, and pulled muscles were common. Like all the starters, Chamique had her share of injuries.

Finally, the regular season ended and the playoffs began. The Lady Vols won their first games to compete in the Elite Eight in San Jose, California, from which the Final Four would be chosen. Games among the Final Four would decide who would emerge as the national champions. Could Tennessee make it their fourth championship?

"Defeat" was not a word in Chamique's vocabulary until a disastrous loss to Duke University. Bowing her head and on the verge of tears at a news conference, she had to acknowledge that Tennessee would not win its fourth national championship.

Having gone through three tournaments, Chamique knew how rough the action could be in the playoffs—much rougher than in the regular season. She was used to playing through the pain of knotted muscles and ignoring the bumps and bruises from close contact under the hoop. In the past, her endurance had been rewarded with victory for the Lady Vols.

This time, however, her dream of another national championship was shattered when Duke University overcame the Tennessee team. Missing shot after shot at the hoop, Chamique scored only eight points. She had suffered her first taste of defeat and was in tears by the end of the game. For the first time, she had to watch another team cut down the net (a basketball tradition for the winning team).

Although Chamique would not play in the finals, she stayed in San Jose, where she did have the pleasure of receiving well-deserved awards. She was named to the Kodak All-American team for the fourth time as well as being named to the Kodak Silver Anniversary Team as one of the best basketball players of the past 25 years. Later that same day, the AP awarded her the Player of the Year honor for the second straight year.

On the very next day, Friday, Chamique also accepted the Division I Player of the Year honor from the Women's Basketball Coaches Association. Overwhelmed with emotion and speaking from her heart, Chamique closed her acceptance speech with the words "It has been a great run, and I've had a good, good career. And I want to thank everyone for really supporting me in my quest to take women's basketball to another level."

The following Sunday, the U.S. Basketball Writers Association gave Chamique its Player of the Year award. Everywhere she went that week, admirers crowded around, congratulating her and clamoring for her autograph. One woman jumped on the stage after an awards ceremony to shake her hand. "I think you are the best player ever," the fan exclaimed. A reporter asked Chamique if that happened a lot. "Yeah, kind of. But it's OK," she said humbly.

For the first time in her incredible college career, Chamique finally realized what she had actually achieved. From her numerous television appearances, everybody seemed to know

AS SELECTED BY THE WBCA

As one of the top 10 women basketball players of 1999, Chamique (back row center) poses with fellow players who were named to the Division I Kodak All-America team. Chamique was only one of three players to receive this honor four times.

this young champion. People who may have never have noticed a woman college player before now recognized her wherever she went. Reporters and fans followed her around as they might pursue a rock star.

Modest and unassuming, Chamique was not about to let the attention go to her head. Grandmother Holdsclaw had not brought her up to brag about her achievements. Chamique did not take credit for what she had done. "It's a blessing, all a blessing," she said.

On May 14, 1999, Chamique received one more award. It was not for her accomplishments on the court but for her hard work in the classroom. June Holdsclaw looked on with pride as Chamique crossed the stage to receive her bachelor's degree in political science. One dream had been realized—the skinny little kid from the projects was now a college graduate.

Chamique had no time to rest, however. Having reached the pinnacle of college success, she was about to begin all over again—this time as a rookie in the WNBA.

Would her past winning skills carry her through a future in the tough professional league?

5

A Different
Kind of Game

Professional basketball teams choose their new players in the same way as pro football teams—through a draft. The WNBA begins its draft in early May, and the WNBA team with the worst record in the league picks first. A team can ask for any player from among those who are free to sign a contract at the time. Some are professionals already on WNBA teams whose contracts are about to expire. Others, like Chamique, are college basketball stars.

The 1999 draft was held in New York City on May 4, and just 10 days before Chamique graduated, the picks were announced. Twelve college players were in the four-round draft, and Chamique was the only one to be chosen in the first round. It was official: Chamique would play for the Mystics of Washington, D.C.

The New York Liberty had desperately wanted Chamique. She was the most sought-after collegiate player, and it was clear that she would attract hordes of fans. When the Liberty tried to persuade the Mystics to trade Chamique for other players, it was no deal. The Mystics were not going to

With her new Washington Mystics jersey, Chamique poses with WNBA president Val Ackerman. Being part of a professional team was a different but exciting experience for the young college star, who soon caused a sensation among basketball fans.

let a champion go.

Chamique was not unhappy with the selection. She would be three hours by train from New York, so she would not have the pressure of playing at home but was close enough to visit her grandmother as often as possible. "I'm really excited about going to Washington," she told a reporter after the draft. "I am excited about the fan support. Washington is number one in attendance and I am used to playing in front of a lot of people. . . . Now we just have to win more games."

In a live Internet chat with fans on the same day, Chamique wrote, "It feels great to be picked No. 1 and just to have the chance to do something I love as a professional is a dream come true."

How did Chamique's grandmother feel about her becoming professional? June told an interviewer, "From eighth grade to now, she was always a winner. She just thought it always belonged to you. I told her, 'This is the real world now. You're not going to be under Pat [Summitt]. You have to learn a lot.'"

One thing Chamique would have to learn was to adjust to a different time schedule. Traditionally, basketball is played in the winter months with playoffs in the spring. The game's inventor, James Naismith, wanted to provide an indoor sport during the cold weather months. The WNBA changed that by beginning its season in the summer with playoffs in the fall. By playing in the summer, the WNBA reasoned that its games would attract sports fans who had no men's basketball or football to watch. Apparently it was a wise decision. By summer 1999, fans were crowding arenas to watch women's basketball.

Working on a different time schedule was just one of the adjustments Chamique had to make as a professional player. In college, she had played against different teams from around the country; in the WNBA she would be playing the same teams again and again, and there would be little time between games. Chamique also realized that she would have to play even harder as a pro. In college she had faced teams that might have only one outstanding player; in the WNBA all the players had exceptional talents.

The Washington Mystics are in the WNBA's Eastern Division, which includes Charlotte, North Carolina; Detroit, Michigan; Orlando, Florida; and New York City. The Western Division comprises teams from Houston, Texas; Los Angeles and Sacramento, California; Phoenix, Arizona; and the states of Minnesota and Utah. The teams from each division, or conference, hold playoffs to decide which three will play WNBA championship games.

Eight days after graduation, Chamique was back in a basketball uniform again and about to play her first official professional game against the Charlotte Sting. Could Chamique play as well and as hard against seasoned professionals as she had in her college career? It didn't take long to find out. On June 10, Chamique scored 18 points and pulled down six rebounds, although her team lost to the Sting.

Four days later, the Mystics were in Madison Square Garden to play the New York Liberty, the team Chamique had once hoped to join. "I am excited and feel blessed to play in front of my family and friends," she told reporters before the game. "I also feel a sense of urgency to win a game."

Chamique never let up in her first year with the Mystics. Playing against seasoned professionals, she showed her championship style by grabbing six rebounds and scoring 18 points in her first pro game.

Chamique then went on to score 20 points and a game-high nine rebounds in the Mystics' surprise 83-61 victory over the best team in the Eastern Division. "This is one to build on," she said after the game. "We played with so much emotion and I feel special."

On June 19, against the Orlando Miracle, Chamique had a game-high 23 points, 10 rebounds, and 4 assists. Less than a week later, she stormed through the Houston Comets with a team-high 24 points, plus 6 rebounds and 4 assists. On July 6, she was named Player of the Week for games played from June 28 through July 4, and in two games that same week, she averaged 21.5 points, a league-leading 11.5 rebounds, and 5.5 assists per game. Years of practice shooting basket after basket paid off when she made more than half of her regular shots and nearly 92 percent of her foul shots from the free-throw line.

Because of her exciting play, the Eastern Division chose the rookie as a starting forward in the WNBA's All-Star game at Madison Square Garden against the Western Division on July 14. Before the game, Val Ackerman, president of the WNBA, spoke to the media about the importance of this game to women's basketball: "This is a very important event for our league. . . ." she said. "You're going to see tonight so many things that have come to be symbolic . . . of the WNBA, with great teamwork by our players, incredible sportsmanship, great enthusiasm and passion by the players and the fans."

Every seat in the Garden was filled as the game began. For many fans the most exciting moment came when Chamique and Sheryl Swoopes of the Houston Comets collided on the floor.

Swoopes, an outstanding player and the top vote-getter in the All-Star selections for this first game, is immensely popular. Chamique too is a fan favorite. Although Chamique had admired Sheryl for a long time, there is some rivalry between them, and Swoopes had gotten tired of all the attention poured on Chamique. Before the game, Swoopes complained, "I'm sick of hearing about Chamique Holdsclaw.

Whenever Chamique plays, she attracts enthusiastic fans as well as the frantic attention of the media. Thanks to her and other star players, women's basketball has become a truly national sport.

There are other players in this league."

According to the same writer, however, in that game Chamique lived up to her "billing and hype." Unfortunately, it was the shortest game she had ever played. With only three minutes on the clock, she injured her left hand, breaking an index finger, and she was benched for the second half. The Eastern Division lost the game 79-61.

The first WNBA All-Star game was a showcase for women's basketball, proving that fans enjoyed watching a great game by women players. Although women basketball players were the first to be noticed, they would not be the last. Less than a week after the All-Star game, the U.S. National Women's Soccer Team won the World Cup, putting the spotlight on another aspect of women's sports. The soccer win proved that when women are given the chance, they can excel in a number of sports.

Although the Mystics did not win every game, Chamique continued her incredible play. In August, she was again named WNBA Player of the Week for games played August 2 through August 8, having led the Mystics to a 4-0 record during that time. She averaged 22 points while making 36 of 63 shots she took from the floor. In four games, she took 28 rebounds and blocked seven shots. She also grabbed the ball for five steals. Having won 10 games and lost 17, the Mystics hoped to gain a spot in the Eastern Conference playoffs.

With Chamique's help, the Mystics finished the regular season in fifth place among the six teams in the league, with 12 wins and 20 defeats. It could not be called an astounding record, but it was an improvement over the previous year. In fact, Chamique led the Mystics to four times as many winning games as the team had in 1998. She had every intention of boosting the team to even more victories in the 2000 season.

6

WINNING WAYS

A nn Meyers, an analyst for the NBC/ESPN network, has said of Chamique that "The mark of a great player is, 'Can you score zero points and still make a difference?' Chamique can do that."

Few experts doubt that Chamique can indeed "do that." She is one of the most outstanding players in women's basketball. Some even contend that she is the best player ever—man or woman. Certainly she has the athletic abilities, talent, desire, and determination to take her game to the top. Perhaps more important, however, Chamique is a champion off the court as well as on.

She is modest about her achievements and is not overly impressed with her own importance. No doubt her grandmother gave Chamique a good start and helps keep her on an even keel. "I always tell her: 'Chamique, stay humble,'" June Holdsclaw told a reporter in April 1999, when everyone was praising Chamique's talents. "I would just like her to stay humble, put God first and stay healthy. I don't want all this to go to her head."

Chamique does not only reserve her winning ways for the court. Whether signing autographs for fans or visiting her old neighborhood to encourage young athletes, she is a role model for young people who want to accomplish their dreams.

That same month, *Life* magazine followed Chamique when she returned to her old neighborhood. When she grew up there, the boys tried to play like their heroes—Kareem Abdul-Jabar, Dr. J., Magic Johnson, Larry Bird, and Michael Jordan. They too hoped to play some day in big-time basketball. Now, when Chamique walks down the streets of Astoria and visits the young people's sports clubs, the girls have a hero to look up to and admire.

Chamique is delighted and proud to be their role model. The girls gather around her, calling, "What's up, Chamique?" She is one of their own from the project courts, and she has proved that girls as well as boys can have dreams and turn them into reality.

Not only does Chamique take time out from her busy schedule to encourage girls and young women in her old neighborhood, she has also taken part in a WNBA weekly teleconference, in which fans call in with questions. Chamique's responses made it clear that she was more concerned that her team win games than she was with gaining more honors for herself. She was proud to say that the Mystics were playing as a team, "and we trust each other a little bit more."

One caller wanted to know if she wasn't tired from playing so many games nonstop. "Not at all," she answered. "I feel like I'm in the best shape of my life. It's crunch time . . . when the real champions come to the table. I can't be thinking I'm tired now. I know that my team needs me and I have to go out there and try to perform."

Another asked how she had handled the pressure of coming into the league after college. "I don't think it's really been anything to handle. You know, you just go out there and try to win

games and just play basketball and that's what my focus is. . . . It's just about being comfortable with myself and comfortable with this team."

When one fan asked if Chamique had ever thought of doing anything else after college other than playing basketball, she quoted her grandmother: "Chamique, you have nice taste, you like nice things, so until you can afford those things, you need to stay in school." Then Chamique added, "You know, I thought about if I wasn't playing basketball, what would I be doing? I probably would be in law school."

Smiling broadly and waving to the crowd, Chamique and her Mystics teammates celebrate a win. Although she won honors in her first year with the team, Chamique does not feel that her personal awards are as important as leading her team to victory.

How did Chamique feel about being on a team that wasn't on top? asked one caller. She admitted that it was hard at first, "but I realized I'm going to have to go through some growing pains. I've been spoiled. I guess I've always endured a lot of success, but losing that championship in college was probably the best thing for me . . . in order to encounter a lot of success, God's going to have to see how you handle the failure."

Asked what she did to relax, Chamique said she likes to go to amusement parks and movies and "hang with my close friends." She added that she doesn't have many friends. "My grandmother always told me, 'If you have one that's good enough.'"

When the subject of the 2000 Olympic Games came up, Chamique made her feelings clear. "If I am a part of that then that's definitely going to be a dream come true and something that I'm very interested in." Then she was asked how long she had been dreaming about the Olympics. "Since I was young," she replied, "it was always something I wanted to do."

Another fan asked Chamique how important it would be for her to win a medal. "It would really be exciting. I guess I've been teased with my World Championship gold medal with the qualifying team. Just to be an Olympian and win the gold medal would be a dream come true. I might even cry."

Two days after answering her fans' many questions, Chamique had the opportunity to cry. She had been named to the U.S. Women's National Basketball Team and would be on the 10-member squad representing the United States in the 2000 Olympics in Sydney, Australia.

Chamique (second from left) proudly displays the jersey she will wear for Team USA in the 2000 Olympics. Although she and her teammates face a hectic schedule of practice and play to prepare for the games, playing in the Olympics is a dream come true for Chamique. She is determined to win a gold medal.

Less than two weeks after that teleconference, Chamique added another honor to her professional career. She was named the 1999 WNBA Rookie of the Year, winning the award after receiving 48 votes out of a possible 51 from a panel of sportswriters and broadcasters. In her first season as a professional player, Chamique Holdsclaw had averaged 16.9 points, 7.9 rebounds, and 2.4 assists. She also played an average of 34.2 minutes of every 40-minute game. She started 31 of 32 games and was the sixth-best scorer and third-best rebounder in only her first season with the WNBA

Chamique knows what it means to be a winner and an inspiration to others. As long as she has anything to do with it, the United States will bring home an Olympic medal in women's basketball and her Washington Mystics will be champions.

STATISTICS

COLLEGE

Year	Team	G	FGM	FGA	Pct.	FTM	FTA	Pct.	REB	AST	PTS	AVG
1995–96	Tenn	36	237	507	.468	102	143	.713	326	75	583	16.2
1996–97	Tenn	39	332	667	.498	122	183	.667	367	114	803	20.6
1997–98	Tenn	39	370	678	.546	166	217	.765	328	117	915	23.5
1998–99	Tenn	34	294	567	.519	133	188	.707	274	80	724	21.3
TOTALS		148	1233	2419	.510	523	731	.715	1295	386	3025	20.4

USA

Year	Competition	G	FGM	FGA	Pct.	FTM	FTA	Pct.	REB	AST	PTS	AVG
1995	USOFE	4	15	29	.517	8	12	.667	21	5	40	10.0
1997	WCQ	5	39	57	.539	16	18	.889	31	1	95	19.0
1997	WCQP	13	69	125	.552	32	44	.727	84	11	170	13.1
1998	WC	9	38	82	.463	22	36	.611	49	10	98	10.9
1998	WCP	6	22	45	.489	12	18	.667	37	8	57	9.5
TOTALS		37	183	338	.541	90	128	.703	222	35	460	12.4

WNBA

Year	Team	G	FGM	FGA	Pct.	FTM	FTA	Pct.	REB	AST	PTS	AVG
1999	Washington	31	202	462	.437	116	150	.773	246	74	525	16.9

G	Games Played	PTS	Points
FGM	Field Goals Made	AVG	Average
FGA	Field Goals Attempted	USOFE	U.S. Olympic Festival-East
Pct.	Percentage	WC	World Championship
FTM	Free Throws Made	WCP	Pre-World Championship
FTA	Free Throws Attempted	WCQ	World Championship Qualifying
REB	Rebounds	WCQP	Pre-World Championship Qualifying
AST	Assists		

CHRONOLOGY

1977   Born on August 9 in Queens, New York

1988   Parents separate; moves in with grandmother, June Holdsclaw

1990–91   Plays for championship Lutheran Grammar School team in New York City

1991–95   Plays for Christ the King High School in New York; wins New York State championship four years in a row

1996   Plays for the University of Tennessee Lady Vols; wins NCAA Championship; is the only freshman chosen as one of 10 Kodak All-Americans

1997   Wins NCAA championship; is named Kodak All-American; is named Most Valuable Player of Final Four in NCAA tournament

1998   Wins NCAA Championship; is named Kodak All-American; becomes Most Valuable Player; wins prestigious James E. Sullivan Memorial Award; earns a gold medal in the World Championships

1999   Graduates from University of Tennessee with B.A. degree; joins Washington Mystics as first choice in WNBA draft; chosen to play in the first WNBA All-Star game; named WNBA Rookie of the Year; selected for U.S. Women's National Basketball Team for 2000 Olympics

FURTHER READING

Barovick, Harriet. "The Meek Shall Inherit." *Time, March 22, 1999.*

Kaminker, Laura. "The World's Best Player?" *Sports Illustrated for Kids,* February 12, 1998.

Samuels, Allison, and Mark Starr. "She's Got Her Own Game." *Newsweek,* March 15, 1999.

"She's Got Next." *Life,* April 1999.

Summitt, Pat. *Reach for the Summitt.* New York: Broadway Books, 1998.

———. *Raise the Roof.* New York: Broadway Books, 1999.

ABOUT THE AUTHOR

Former English teacher KAY CORNELIUS is a full-time freelance writer who lives in Huntsville, Alabama. She likes to study and write about history and has written magazine articels, short stories, one novella, and nine novels, most about history. *Chamique Holdsclaw* is her second children's book. The other is *The Supreme Court*, also for Chelsea House.

HANNAH STORM, NBC Sports play-by-play announcer, reporter, and studio host, made her debut in 1992 at Wimbledon during the All England Tennis Championships. Shortly thereafter, she was paired with Jim Lampley to cohost the *Olympic Show* for the 1992 Olympic Games in Barcelona. Later that year, Storm was named cohost of *Notre Dame Saturday*, NBC's college football pregame show. Adding to her repertoire, Storm became a reporter for the 1994 Major League All-Star Game and the pregame host for the 1995, 1997, and 1999 World Series. Storm's success as host of *NBA Showtime* during the 1997-98 season won her the role as studio host for the inaugural season of the Women's National Basketball Association in 1998.

In 1996, Storm was selected as NBC's host for the Summer Olympics in Atlanta, and she has been named as host for both the 2000 Summer Olympics in Sydney and the 2002 Winter Olympics in Salt Lake City. Storm received a Gracie Allen Award for Outstanding Personal Achievement, which was presented by the American Women in Radio and Television Foundation (AWRTF), for her coverage of the 1999 NBA Finals and 1999 World Series. She has been married to NBC Sports broadcaster Dan Hicks since 1994. They have two daughters.

INDEX

Ackerman, Val, 51

All-American Red Heads, 12

AP Player of the Year, 34, 43

Artest, Ron, 20

Boys and Girls Club, 18, 20

Cannizzaro, Vincent, 20, 21, 30

Catchings, Tamika, 33

Charlotte Sting, 49

Christ the King High School, 12-13, 20-22

Eastern Division, 49, 50, 51-52, 53

ESPN Player of the Week, 28

Final Four Most Valuable Player, 31, 34

Green, Tyrone, 18, 20

Holdsclaw, Chamique
  birth of, 17
  childhood of, 15, 17-20, 56
  and education, 12-13, 14-15, 18, 19, 20-23, 25-28, 30-31, 33-35, 37-45, 58
  family of, 17-19
  as professional, 33, 39-40, 45, 47-49
  as role model, 55-56

Holdsclaw, Davon (brother), 17

Holdsclaw, June (grandmother), 10, 17-19, 20, 22, 23, 30-31, 33, 39-40, 44, 48, 55, 57, 58

Honda-Broderick Cup, 13, 34

Houston Comets, 50-51

James E. Sullivan Memorial Award, 13-14, 34

Jordan, Michael, 9-10, 12, 13, 14-15

Kodak All-American team, 13, 28, 31, 43

Kodak Silver Anniversary Team, 13

Kona Classic Most Valuable Player, 30

Lady Vols, 25-28, 30-31, 33-35, 37-45

Meyers, Ann, 55

Naismith, James, 13, 48

Naismith Player of the Year Award, 13

NCAA Championship, 28, 31, 34, 41-43, 58

New York Liberty, 39-40, 47, 49-50

New York State High School Championships, 13, 21

Olympics, 12, 13, 58, 59

Orlando Miracle, 50

Southeastern Conference Player of the Week, 28

Summitt, Pat, 14-15, 22, 26, 27-28, 30-31, 33-34, 37, 39, 48

Swoopes, Sheryl, 51-52

U.S. Basketball Writers Association Player of the Year, 13, 43

University of Tennessee, 14-15, 22-23, 25-28, 30-31, 33-35, 37-45, 58

Washington Mystics, 14, 47-51, 53, 56, 58, 59

Western Division, 49, 51

WNBA All-Star game, 51-52

WNBA Player of the Week, 51, 53

WNBA Rookie of the Year, 59

WNBA weekly teleconference, 56-58

Women's Basketball Coaches Association Division I Player of the Year, 43

Women's National Basketball Association (WNBA), 12, 14, 39, 45, 47, 48-49, 51, 59

World Basketball Championships, 13, 34, 58